GIFTS FROM A QUILL

Winning Poems Anthology

INTRODUCTION

Gifts from a Quill

We come as worshippers of desires,
Bringing with us these offerings of words.
We have come from the tetrad spheres of breath,
Sailing the seven seas of inspiration.
Though we have different shades of skin,
The colour of our inks blend with pristine perfection.

Let the altar of contemplation
Be prepared to receive these fattened lambs of thought.
We have dipped our the quill of imagination
In the filled bottle of rhymes, rhythm and diction.
We have mated the virgin pages of artistry
With the fairest feather of fantasy.

We do not claim to be spotless sages;
We have not fully dipped our souls in the waters of Hippocrene.
We do not reside fully within the borders of Elysian Plane.
But let these be known to the altars
Upon which will burn our sacrifices:
For it is our very hearts which dance on the pages!
It's the fire of our unbridled passion
Which burns through these lively bones of words?

Written and Copyright by;
Marvin Omosemen
Resident judge of POETRY PLANET

ADMINISTRATORS AND MODERATORS

Lovely Garcia
Administrator/Founder
Lovely is the founder of POETRY PLANET, a study group that helps build new writers through poetry competitions. She has published book anthologies and books from International writers. Her mission in life is to help aspiring poets to become published writers. She lives by the motto: "I may have failed to fulfill my dream, but I was able to fulfill the dreams of others". Read her poem on page 107.

Christy Hall-Hollowell
Moderator
Christy was born in NC. As a child, Christy's aunt encouraged her to write in order to get her feelings out, which began the journey into poetry, leading to a way to overcome adversities. Now, Christy is married, with two children. She enjoys writing, painting, reading, and spending time with her family. Motto- Use today, tomorrow isn't promised. Read her poem on page 107.

Marites Quindoza Tordecilla
Moderator
Marites is born in Gumaca, Quezon and graduated in Bachelor of Science in Accountancy in Polytechnic University of the Philippines. A loving mom, farm secretary, and an accountant. Working and living on a farm inspired her to write about love, hope, dream, and nature." Read her poem on 112.

Tanushi Singh
Moderator
Tanushi is a Structural Engineer by profession but a poetess at heart. She seeks poetry to speak her soul. Poetry is her creative outlet to celebrate life. A firm believer in the power of words. Through her blog on Facebook 'Create Believe Inspire ', where she writes on love, life and motivation. She hopes to inspire others to believe in their dreams. Read her poem on page 109.

BOARD OF JUDGES

Ruth Joy Darling
Judge

Ruth is a busy wife, career woman and a mother of three, Ruth believes she has the best of both worlds: a stable career and the time to dabble in poetry. An avid reader since childhood, she always borrowed poetry books from the High School library, especially those written by famous poets such as Shakespeare, Frost, Robert and Elizabeth Browning.

Marvin Omosemen
Judge

Benson is a Life Coach, Motivational Speaker, Pastor, Author, and Poet. He has written some books, the most recent being a motivational piece titled WORDS OF LIFE FOR A LIFE. He lives in Lagos, Nigeria. He is married to Chidinma Benson, and they are blessed with two lovely kids.

Maria Dulce Leitao Reis
Judge

In this meaningful journey, Maria Dulce Leitão Reis captivates us with a delectable compendium of poems conveying her observances of our society through her very own experiences. She does not shy away from taking us through the whole gambit of living in our world and in so doing vividly reflects our vicissitudes through the mirror of her pen.

GRAPHIC ARTISTS

Saswat Kumar Mishra

Banner Maker

Saswat Kumar Mishra is a young boy with highly creative spirit. His passion for digital art has been noteworthy through the numerous banners he continues to create for Poetry Planet tirelessly. He is a humble artist with great potential. Saswat is also passionate about photography and has created a Facebook page called International Mobile Click Photography to showcase his photography talent.

He is multifaceted boy who inks poetry for living simple joys, a true aspiring artist who can grow to achieve great heights. Read his poem in 111.

Nath Villacorte

Banner Maker

Elnard "Nath" Villacorte is born March 05, 1993 in Naga, Zamboanga Sibugay, Philippines. A silent-type writer, who loves writing poems to inspire other people, art design, is also one of his hobbies. An amateur in photographic art but his dedication is seen by the beauty of his creations that a member of Poetry Planet was able to appreciate.

INDEX

THE GIFTED POETS

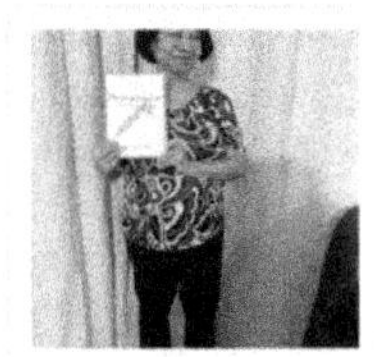

''To build a strong foundation, one should dedicate his heart and soul and commitment. My passion and vision to assist aspirants in their pathway to success will continue, even during times of hardships and difficulties...''

Lovely Garcia
Publisher/Founder

FINALLY

So many sad songs filled my cold heart
Then flowed freely like a moving art
Beneath the glorious sunset dance
The sun, the sea, and sky took a chance
With me, and I, with you quick thinking
It might be you that I am seeking,

All this time and all the soft kisses
And all the warm hugs this world misses
Shall shine on my feelings day and night,
Brightening my dreams, spreading the light
In my dark mind, all the while thinking
It might be you I have been yearning,

All this time you have made me happy
In the most beauteous way, deeply
You carved my soul in pure ecstasy,
And painted sweet serendipity
Upon my parched lips, while whispering
You love me. Now, I am done searching.

Copyright by LJ V Madrazo ©2018

I FOUND YOU

Somewhere out there from the billion of stars,
A meteor has fallen appearing as a streak of light sparks,
Brightens my gloomy and dark stormy night,
Like a glistering dew of promising sunlight...
Which enters in the phrases of my unvarnished poem?
Arranging those messy words and unrythmic locution,
Garnishing it with care along with proper rhythm,
With pinch of admiration and a scoop of attention...
Who runs before me while walking in the vast,
Clearing up those hurdles that cause stumbling block,
Cleaning my path of life that was disorganized,
Wiping these weary eyes where tears never depart...
Maybe you are, who always roam in my dreams,
The one who ignites the long been faded flame
Fueling the heat that frozen by cold wind,
Thawing this frosty heart, teaching to love again...

Copyright by Jaguar Ti tambuli

IS IT REALLY CHRISTMAS

Did you feel the gentle touch of winter season,
Reminding the time of fun and celebration?

No! What you feel is the embrace of love and peacefulness,
The caring and affection with hope and happiness.

Did you hear the noise of children in the streets,
With their out of tune voices singing on Christmas Hymns?

No! What you're hearing is the spirit of gladness,
An innocent laughter and joy so naive and guileless.

Have you notice the sounds of trumpet and cymbals,
Together with the drums, tambourine and guitars?

No! What you've notice is act of celebration,
Commemoration of prophesied child was born.

Have you seen the art, formed by fireworks in the sky,
Brightens the dark nights like twinkling little stars?

No! What you've seen is hope that promised in this future,
Salvation of souls by our beloved saviour.

What are those presents mean under the Christmas tree?
Are those gifts come from heart, or just a giveaway?

What a luxurious foods so lavish on display
Neglecting the poor's ordeal and difficulty!

Christmas must not be fixed on a season or time,
But all year round, it should be our state of mind.

The true spirit of Christmas must come from our hearts,
Follow the lead of Jesus, spread peace, hope, love and light!

Copyright by Jaguar Ti Tambuli

Road of divine glow
Unveils the dawning twilight
Smiling at orbit

Copyright by Albert Juniho Onwuchekwa

Aureole dazzles
Rainbow spectrum enlivened
On canvas of snow

Copyright by Purbasha Roy

Clouds, sky, snow and trees--
All bathe in faint orange glow
Winter sun awakes!

Copyright by LJ V Madrazo

DAMSEL LANE

Today it seems life is fading down
Pediments of blue hills wear playful sunshine crown

I took journey of my damsel lane long left behind
That holds your fragrance in withered blossoms rustling wild

The path less trodden developed silence of rusted time
Waiting to be broken with forgotten damsel chime

Peeling off the shroud from the frosty skies
Tracking out fondness spread in thousand miles

Each damp step rises Petrich or beneath feet's
Awakened soul yearns for its share of love's ripened feast

Empty forest boughs has remains of dreams nest
Indigo clouds gaze with agony at fading west

Alone and waiting for endless hours
Memories fall as amber leaves in damsel mischievous showers

Nomadic damsel tale that screams in muffled echoes
Looks for shelter at heart's fawn meadows

In illusion of time silhouette of shadows and light
Cowering fast with splurge of black on white

Wandering to inhale lost scent of blooming buds
In trembling anticipation of dripping unheard words

Traversing through streams of rippling hopes
Trying to untangle weaker joints of adulthood's tight ropes

Patina of anguish in turnings misleads from the exit
To forever wander with crawling steps in exile

Copyright by Purbasha Roy

LOVERS WITH BENEFIT

The slowly rising moon speaks,
The glowing light spreads.
The love that was to come,
With the benefits all along.

After a long separation,
Getting a respite of union.
It is lovers benefit now,
To forgo all miseries somehow.

The life blesses a few good moments,
Of together ness pleasant.
Cravings are calmed with exchange,
Of the talks that still remained.

In calm so rounding of ocean,
Golden rays all around blossom...
Here are lovers with benefit,
In the serene golden outfit.

Copyright by Shailendra Kr Singh

."

SOME LOVE

Some love begins when another ends!
Mine started when I caught you stealing
Furtive glances at me in an old friend's
Boring party as you were leaving,

Next thing I knew, we were in the car
Talking anything under the star,
In your eyes, I can see a woman
In need of an occasional man

Who will fill the void of failed marriage
And let you escape the prison cage,
More than a friend less than a lover
That will rain your parched Indian summer,

Under the waxing moon, we promised
If neither of us could be honest
Of the secret lives within our skin
Then, our great love ends with another sin.

Copyright by LJ V MADRAZO

SPRING

If we sow our love
Will you tend with me our hearts?
I yearn to bloom here with you

We'll grow with our love
Fragrant blossoms adorn us
Flowering eternally

Copyright by Jodi Matenga

OOF AGE AND BEAUTY

Life's wrinkles may show
Endless up and down cycle
In the journey of all men

But time can't erase
The heart's genuine beauty—
To truly love and be loved!

Copyright by LJ V Madrazo

THE WILL

Mortals say my dreams are too great
That the paths I've chosen to mate
Have thorns which even gods feet grate.

But let both gods and men with shame behold
These maddened feet of mine tread realms untold,
Bearing the compass of a soul unsold!
The reed kneels at the feeble call of doom
The sun sinks in the heartless hands of gloom
And blossoms buried in autumnal tombs!

But I'm the rose that sprouts from soulless wombs of stone!
I'm the bold youth who makes the giant's head his own!
I'm the lone wheat amidst the thorns, seeking the throne!
I'm the hungry altar that beckons flames to fly!
I'm the Northern Star smiling in the Western sky!
I'm the steely ship assail dark waters that cry!
I'm the heart brave that falls not in love with the grave!
I'm the camel who to thirst is never a slave!
I'm the wind with a mind that none can ever stave!

Copyright by Marvin Omosemen

INESCAPABLE

Behind the veil of past, you came
Weeping, you called for my lost name
But things will never be the same.

You traced my name under the gathered dust
But what I saw are roads of wanderlust
Leading us back to the place of mistrust
After you left me broken and shaken
Forsaken and totally forgotten
What else is worse that could ever happen?

Softly, you whispered my name in the wind hoping
The rivers will cease flowing, mountains from growing,
Hills from rolling and the old forest from spreading
But even if all these absurd things came to pass
How is life's certainty looking under the glass?
Wouldn't it be better off to lie amongst the grass?
And under the crescent moon dream of tomorrow
With a fresh set of eyes that haven't seen deep sorrow
Knowing the will of the wind can always follow?

Copyright by LJ V Madrazo

Untitled

Love me through the phone
Kiss me as if u were home
We are far, but not alone

Copyright by Angela Saucedo

FACE TO FACE

Face to face we are
Though our loving lips don't touch
Darling, I'm always with you

Copyright by Rose Huy Woolket

YOU DEFINE STARDUST

We all are made of stardust is all that I know
But why does no one possess this aureate glow
Other than you who has the beauty so divine
Or the freshness much soughed in cool drinks of lime
The whole choir of angels seems to sing melodies
Admiring your rainbow beauty in reveries
Ripples emerald vales get as you sit near them
Stardust falls from your caramel cheeks in night's thrum
You are the queen of surreal meadows in blooms
Fathomless fantasy of burning candle plumes
I feel I had known you since centuries ago
When God created love with stardust sprinkling low
You are resplendent oasis in life's sand dunes
Stardust gets its worth spanned in your cherubic tunes
You define stardust in most exuberant way
Scarlet poem with darning's of emotions play.

Copyright by Purbasha Roy

THE REVELATION

Underneath the sweet hush of the dusky twilight
Gorgeous stardust's unravel in pure fancy flight
The new moon gave birth to a billion stars tonight
And like playful fireflies with enchanting soft light
Entices lovers to send their secret wishes
In the midst of this beautiful chaos arose
Countless of meteor showers magical shows
Dotting the great ocean of swirling galaxies
As if moving all in the same symphonic rhythm
Then gently guided by God's cryptic algorithm
Happiness consumed the awakened universe
Inspiring flowing and rhyming melodic verse
To spring forth out of the young poet's immortal pen
Providing heavenly inspiration to men
And for all ages to come, will serve to remind
That we're all constellation in His cosmic mind.

Copyright by LJ V Madrazo

DISTANT MEMORIES

Distant memories haunt my mind
Flash backs of moments so unkind
Keep digging, who knows what you'll find
Tears fall on the blade of a knife
Now dripping crimson colored life
My mind is full of pain and strife.

Exhausted, disconnected from my soul
Tired, broken, the world has taken its toll
Under the moonlight I watched the smoke roll
Helpless tears fall from a reflected eye
Staring out my window I sit and cry
Left destroyed I ask the universe, why?

Crickets chirping, the embers drifting to the ground
Memories stir emotion not normally found
You're screaming, and I cower not making a sound
I have distant memories, and vivid nightmares
Scared child seeking help, in a closet through prayer
A stolen childhood, sadly you don't seem to care...

Copyright by Savannah Hargis

I had it all once
Or did I, money and peace
A Piece of money

Copyright by Marion Parish

Show me your money
And I will show you knowledge
Ignorance is free

Copyright by Rose Diaz

Only the smartest
Will gain a proper foothold...
Maybe the dumbest?

Copyright by Micheal King

CAMOUFLAGE

Rain drops every night
With no stars overhead
No moon to light the flood
That's slowly drowning up my head.

The World is truly cruel
For it's what made me feel alone
Life was kicking me away
Telling me that I don't belong.

But as time flies
Days go by
I've learnt new things
I've learnt to smile.

It served me both
As Shield and Sword
It also helped me
Blend in to this World.

It was my Armor
It was my all
It was what helped me
Take down towering walls.

But Have I changed?
No, not at all
I just learned how to Camouflage
In this Path I Crawl...

Copyright by Pat Lang

HIDE AND SEEK

Days went by as it always should
Usually, the bad goes with the good
But lately, things seem out of place
When you said that you needed some space.

I really should have known long ago
Signs that said something was not so
But my mind fought what my heart heard
In your most silent unspoken word.

Tonight might be our final dance
Masquerade lost its second chance
Time to let go of the hidden mask
Because in your true face, I will dare ask

If you are in love with somebody else?
Your answer came like broken spells
And your untruthful eyes thus revealed
What your lying lips long concealed.

Copyright by LJ V Madrazo

FALSE LOVE FALLS

Imprisoned by a false love,
Living with no freedom is hard,
Where she learnt to sneak out
Meeting someone whom she truly loves...

But Alas! Her illicit affair has been caught,
Accepting her sad fate without regret
Tortured in her concealment,
Kneeling for survival, day and night.

The Lord opened the door of enlightenment,
She was forgiven and given another chance,
But she chose to leave her arrogant husband
For she can no longer feel safe on his hands.

Who are we to judge her,
If she moved away to feel better,
And find new home with her lover,
Where she find peace and security forever?

Copyright by Jaguar Ti Tambuli

THE FASTEST TRAVELLER...

Just whisper,
Something in an ear,
And look at the eyes
It'd brighten with cheer,
Please don't say it
To anybody else,
Add this at last,
For sure, it would travel
Very very fast...

It's a biting humour,
What's that travels fast
Is certainly a Rumour ...?

Mr. Jones has affair
With Mrs. Leonney,
May it sound fake & funny,
But it goes round and round
With a pace profound,
As if it has wings to fly
From end to end of sky,
Each and every eager ear
Is its precious consumer,
Those make it travel fast
None other than Rumour.

When healthy, it moves slowly
When filthy, it doth glow,
Sometimes high, sometimes low,
It's but always in a flow,
A benign or a malignant
Unavoidable tumour,
Boomer is the Rumour ...

Copyright by Dr. Achyut Kumar Rath

TORN INTO TWO

I love you...
But I love him too
Being polyamorous is part of me
Why is that so hard to see?

It's not wrong, its infinite love
You make me feel torn
On my rose, you are the thorn
But I love you too

If you can't accept that part of me
The part that is wild and free
Then we can no longer be
Because you are blind refusing to see

You can't force me to live your way
And I cannot force you to stay
Sometimes love isn't enough
But who holds your hand when life is rough

I wish you could see the world from my eyes
Torn between two, at night I cry
Why make me regret being honest, should I have lied?
Maybe I'm better without you by my side

Copyright by Savannah Hargis

WHEN YOU LEAVE ME BLUE

As I'm standing early in the morning,
The cloudless sky is so beautiful and stunning,
Wiping my doubts and burdens carrying
As the birds are flying and happily chirping.

As you walk away leaving me so blue
My soul shivers when you sing the song, "Blue Bayou"
How fast could you say we're already through
Feeling sad and lonely, you wave your last adieu!

Like a bird with broken wings in the wild,
With nowhere to go and nobody at my side,
Makes me feel confuse and out of my mind
Trying to find ways to make this anger subside!

Missing those lovely whisper from your heart,
The good inspirational words you have impart,
That was implanted to my deepest part,
The only things left when you suddenly depart...

Copyright by Jaguar Ti Tambuli

HOLDING, BEING

In my arms I hold
You close, warming you with love.
The sun warms us both.
We two transcend the cosmos,
The universe is in us.

Copyright by Paul Hudson

Untitled

These mothers embrace...
A shelter, lacking danger;
A child fears nothing.
Yet in the dark, her hope fades,
Mother is lost to nightmares.

Copyright by Micheal King

CARELESS WHISPER

You're the bud of my blossoming thought
Such a feeling I earnestly sought
Lips tracing maze of juicy feeling
Combusting soul with passionate healing

Our heart syncs at the same pace
Aloft into the skies as we aptly race
Serenading vibes of careless whisper
A soothing balm to soul without blister

Our hearts sing a song called love
In harmony as we transcend above
Into the ethereal of unforgettable bliss
Filled with dews of mellifluous kiss

Two soul entwined in rhythms of rhymes
As we waltz to the thrills of melodious chime
Resonating vibes of sweet memories
That submerged us in the cape of reveries.

© AJ Rhymes 2018
Albert Juniho Onwukchekwa

SOME LEARN WITHIN A YEAR

Some learn within a year
For me, it took, so long and a million tears
You gave me absolutely, nothing but pain
Once more, you say let's start again

Some learn within a year

We shared each other's spirits, during the days
You never could give, you continued to play
I shared my loving, caring heart completely
You gave me loveless lonely, to feel, empty

Some learn within a year

I'll give you, your lonely heart
Love lives, with a new start
There's no more growing grieving
My bags and heart packed, we're leaving

I've learned within this year

Love will have a new start, a new heart, new love

Copyright by Rose Huy Woolket

We too have a place
To nest in this wide, wide world
Of concrete and glass

Copyright by Omar Nassar

On temple or mosque
I will sit without thinking
About religion

Copyright by Sudha Dixit

JUST FOR TONIGHT

Tonight my love,
Our inspired imagination
Will fly us through
The unending horizon
Soaring high above
Hills and mountains
And off to the silvery moon
To chase the dream
We gladly share.

Tonight my love,
We will leave
This depressing reality
With a vanishing trail
Of red rose petals
And there in our crescent world
We will build our own
Emerald garden paradise
Bereft of sadness and pain.

Tonight my love,
We will drink sweet nectar
With the stars of Milky Way
While we synchronize
Our inner galaxies
To pirouette in the infinite vastness
Of the unknown universe
With our heart and soul
In divine harmony.

Copyright by LJ V Madrazo

VENOM

You are the son of ambrosia
In cloudy sky you're the supernova
You're the pioneer for aberrant
Convoys of deviants,

But you forgot your annals
You're one among the noble angels
You are source of nectars
Not the Holocaust of venom's,

Rejuvenated landscape you altered
In the conspiracy of divide and rule policy
Spurring people for wager
Drizzling venom drops in courtyard of sober
You smeared your own dignity and glamour,

Dear recalling glorious history of yours
Leave people to live in peace and pampers
Drifting the source of ambergris
Retrieve your abdicated prerogatives.

Copyright ANUPAMA SAR

MOONLIGHT ROMANCE

There
Upon my sight
The moonlight
With radiant shine
Beams upon mine

Where
I toast my tea
Moon with me
My companion
I, with no one

Rare
Moment events
In a sense
I talk to moon
Ask a great boon

Dare
To moon I say
Light my way
Out of darkness
To happiness

Copyright by Ency Bearis

ANGEL

Incredible feat!
An Angel forming in you?
Amazing heavenly gift

I'll pamper you twice
No way to express my awe
Oh, you've the best baby bump

Copyright by Ngam Emmanuel

Untitled

Leaves watch over us,
As we await the future-
Wondering what you will be.

I will stand watch soon
As the future becomes 'now'-
And I watch you grow and bloom.

Copyright by Marianna Nicole Hill

Untitled

A new life begins
Lives in the womb of thy love
Made out of our flesh and blood

It'll grow to seek love
And to find the other half
For another life to sprout

Copyright by Siegfreid Chadwick

I love how you love
me, in the ocean of love
where every drop knocks

Copyright by Margaret Kowalewska

Let's submerged our love
to this salty water, dear,
Preserved and sealed with a kiss

Copyright by Ency Bearis

SLAVE TO YOU

My love, you are
Moon from afar
I worship in vain
Despite all the pain...

My mind and heart in war
Like a broken guitar
Playing soft and warm refrain
Against never ending rain...

Left with nothing but aching scar
My poor soul seems trapped in a jar
Craving for your endless and cold reign
Giving in to the plainly insane...

As with all things under the wondrous star
None is truer than true love's avatar
To be free and yet to still long for the harsh chain
If that is all it takes to be with you again...

Copyright by LJ V Madrazo

I WILL SURVIVE

I was not born to quit this living death
Though the youngest of dreams has lost its breath!
I'll rise like the sun buried in the west!
I will soar like an eaglet from its nest!

Copyright by Marvin Omosemen

MY BABY'S HOME

I've got a handful of heartache
And my pockets full of dreams
An angel of my shoulder
She's the prettiest thing that I've seen
When she shows me that smile
And she walks out in the dark
She kind of lights my fire
With desire, she's the spark
She's got a style with passion
She's a ten with all the looks
The gender warm and tender
With all the curves and all the hooks
A fashion on the catwalk
Well she's my beauty queen
Stepped out from the pages
Of a sexy magazine
She's got the boys a crawling
And their begging on their knees
A hopeful chance to have a dance
She's burning by degrees
She's as sweet as honey
And I'm a dog without a bone
Cause every time I see her
I thank god my baby's home...

Copyright by Martin Edge

POPULARITY

What does a man gain from Popularity?
Generations come and go with all hostility,
Man toils under the sun consistently,
And we all end up to God's generosity!

Popularity in this World is full of complexity,
Fame is meaningless without God's connectivity,
All things are wearisome and full of adversity,
But life with God is lived... beautifully and amazingly!

Copyright by Gina Gelua

Untitled

You are in wrong line
This doesn't lead to heaven
Try thankfulness queue

Copyright by Margaret Kowalewska

UNGRATEFUL

The glass is half full,
and people complain of thirst,
while they have water.

Copyright by Rusty Brooks

GRATITUDE WITH ATTITUDE

No matter what voice
in volume by the numbers
deaf is blind also...

Copyright by Martin Gedge

MORE THAN A BEAST

Ah! Afraid I was
Lost in the wood of no help
And the falling snow,
Battered me. But a friend came
Looking beastly but soothing.

Copyright by Aboo Ni'mah

Untitled

No words need be spoke
About the bond that we share
Safe in the knowledge
And the comfort you provide
A friend for the rest of time

Copyright by Adam tennant

MORE THAN A BEAST

FRIENDSHIP

Whenever a hand meets another,
With a feeling of going together.

Whenever a heart, known, or unseen.
Comes near to listen to others pain.

When unknown feelings meet each other,
Soothing the mind of one another.

A pact is born, known as friendship,
A picture drawn to see the worship.

Friends know when they are happy,
With the others hard won trophies.

Relation without any gives or take,
Honest feelings real, nothing fake.

Two mind playing in a tune,
Knowing when is other one alone.

When in pain and when in joy,
They all know that goes how.

Intimacy innocent, selfless belonging,
The attachment is just charming.

Real friends have a hard ruling,
They can always die for others asking.

An understanding of unwritten words,
A fellow feeling of two beautiful hearts.

A real friendship knows no laws,
It just sacrifices for other friends flaws.

Immortal, inseparable, and flawless,
Friendship towers over all duress.

©Shailendra Kumar Singh .

.

THE BRILLIANCE

Our love sparkled like a moon
The whispers we talked made the tune

Of untold charm, of the heart warm
The sparkle of smiling arm in arm

The golden aura of sentiments
The eternal silvery beautiful blend

Let's sparkle like pure water
Full of life without a clutter

Let us sparkle like the stars
A face glowing with energy we are

Our world is the glitter of gold
Always young, never going to be old

Let's sparkle like fountain fall
We shall go higher but no turning small

Let's create the glamour together
Of the brightness that we both gathered

We are the sparkle of the universe
We are the shining best ever verse

Copyright by Shailendra Kr Singh

LOCOMOTIVE

Hauling a small train through the ridges
Runs a locomotive crossing little picturesque bridge
Tracks ignited beneath the iron wheels
Dust transiently rise to die down with zeal

Powering way through tunnels and parks
Whistling, filling joy in each eye's spark
Up, up, up, down, down, down
Toy train in the outskirts of the sleepy town

Fading sun upon the horizon smiles
Besides the fruit market everyday it chimes
Attracting tourists from the whole wide world
Running since a century has infinite stories hurled

Who stokes fire to keep it going on and on
Shooting puffed smoky fog from break of dawn
Maintaining the fragile balance through the tracks criss cross
Thrilled shrieks and shouts, flag flogs with wind and sudden toss

Immense strength more than hundred horses spirited
A living vintage tugging hopes and dreams with a hulked body riveting
Propelled with determined grit and blaring horns
It chugged up the swirling path to reach railway yard completely worn

Copyright Purbasha Roy

BREAKER BREAKER

"Breaker Breaker"...this is shaker
There's a Smokey on your tail
And I would suggest to see it best
To dump the junk and bail
He's on your ass and moving fast
So hit the gas and sail
Or keep in mind to spend your time
Inside the county jail
"This is bandit" ...understand it
I've got this in control
My mean machine is full of steam
So watch this sucker blow
I'm about to bust so eat my dust
To make that piggy slow
He isn't a match to even catch
The bandit on the go!!!...

by Martin Gedge
(R.I.P. Burt Reynolds)

GAME

Periwinkle skies
Peekaboo of sun and clouds
Laughs emerald fields

Copyright by Purbasha Roy

A hide-and-seek game
between the light and the shade-
an earthly delight.

Copyright by Kishor Kumar Mishra

In the arms of Light
I bathe eyes with meadows green
and silver of clouds

Copyright by Margaret Kowalewska

Untitled

Just allow me once
To immerse in your dreams, where
Your eyes dance in front of me...

There I'll find myself
I'll find you, and I'll find us
Breathless in closest embrace

Copyright by Margaret Kowalewska

CAVE IN

Thanks for loving me
Though you have a heart of stone
I let it be soft; he says

Your patience is love
No hard stone against the rain
You're rain, I cave in; says she

Copyright by Ency Bearis

Don't be afraid now
Take my hand and cross this bridge
Freedom beckons us

Copyright by Bill Noble

We will meet again
A bridge between two lovers
won't stop my feelings for you

Copyright by Marion Remnant Parish

Follow my heartbeat
Across the bridge of madness
Pausing only for silence

Copyright by David Wells

Why bother with me
My dear. Dead men tell no tales
Send no more flowers.

Copyright by Omar Nassar

Dirt! Don't soil my shroud
Today, only, I took bath
And changed in new clothes

Copyright by Sudha Dixit

CONFUSION OF FEELINGS

Why do I feel I have a soul deluged in confusion?
Is my wandering mind an emblem of allusion
My senses were intact in my conscious decisions
But this splurge of incertitude keeps hammering my wisdom

Thoughts in conflict since a long time
Beyond the comprehensible edges of mine
Losing way to destination on every alternate turn
In this hazy storm it's difficult for me to discern

Sometimes I feel I have finally joined the dots
To realize next moment, I am jumbled up in thoughts
The words fly in mind's skies to crash and fall down
Only to leave a bleak horizon at end of heart's desolate town

I wander to get out of this maze with steps in haste
Only to end up lost, efforts suffocating beneath piled waste
This inquietude that runs through my veins
I missed recognizing the muse entangled in narrow brain's lane

Was I ignorant of all the awareness laid besides?
To lose the rhythm at lowest tide
I need to adjoin fragmented feelings avoiding this squally debate
Without nitpicking pieces of vague ideas to recapitulate

The strenuous task in hand in the unendurable leaking of timepiece
Anxious for recommencement of manifested feelings quiescent

Copyright by Purbasha Roy

Untitled

Bubble bubble me!
With excitement the child plays
Bubble me again!
This magic, with soap all day,
Blowing with glee, in the sun

Copyright by Caroline Adwar

Untitled

A boy's happiness
Blowing bubbles high and low
Flying up above
Gazing upon the meadows
He wonders, where did it go?

Copyright by Jaguar T Tambuli

Misty red roses
Swaying proudly with the wind
Spreading its fragrance

Copyright Mari Felices

Winter rose stands proud
Wearing her veil of snowflakes
Bride of the season

Copyright Lena Power

Untitled

Under the moonlight
And the sounds of nature's bliss,
I gave my beautiful yes

Sealed it with a kiss
Holding hand, tightly embrace
Forever love, I do wish.

Copyright by Mari Felices

Untitled

With her head balanced
On my right breast, my lips thirsts
For an unending soft kiss

Birds singing above,
Moon rays and clouds sparkling bright,
We stand flummoxed between all

Copyright by Njam Theophillus Ghangha

Untitled

You are far, my love
Visit me now in my dream
Let us become one tonight

Echo in my soul
With your sacred love. Let's fly
In the amethysts of skies

Copyright by Margaret Kowalewska

If I only knew
how to read your mind, our life
would become simple for us

Copyright by Margaret Kowalewska

In the silence of
our hearts, we both burn in a
longing faraway from reach.

Copyright by Ojotogba Ugeh

Trees shedding their youth
Fledglings have flown their nest too
Like love between me and you

Copyright by Shilpa Kulkarni

MIRACLE

I have been walking in the dark
For quite some time drifting afar
On long and winding road stark
Down unfamiliar paths for stars

Under dewy hazy foggy sky
A vague notion my wings tied
Bound by some magic spell evil
Wander in meandering lanes feeble

Journey didn't seem to end anywhere
Tempted on adventures somewhere
Hesitant steps onto slightest trails
Distant horizon vanishing affairs

Each call in search of truth guided
The spirit to take flights forward
Traveling to end of Earth misguided
Brought me to my roots backward

In my own arms lay the miracle
Deep down in my soul surrender
In little things love quietly encircle
Simply no words describe such wonder

Copyright by Jyotirmaya Thakur

Stand here to chase me
Let me fart out excrete
To tell you I'm big

Copyright by Njam Theophilus Ghangha

The earth is a place
A place for all you and me
So, live and let live

Copyright by Bipin Churchung Rabha

UNTITLED

So finally he's
Coming back to me truly
After all these years
Why won't I smile again now
When my heart will soon be whole

Copyright by Njam Theophilus Ghangha

HER BEAUTY

She might be giggling
But like music to others
With her smile that shines
Flashes her charm and beauty
Is she beautiful inside?

Copyright by Ency Bearis

A SMILED REFLECTION

A smile reflection
A window gaze looking back
Loving the feeling
Knowing and waiting for me
Tulips pushed against the glass...

Copyright by Martin Gedge

MY GOD

I raise both my hands,
In worship and praise to you,
For your love and grace!

Copyright by Mary Lynn Luiz

Like the lone bright rose
in the midst of white blue clouds
thorns stop no true love

Copyright by Njam Theophilus Ghangha

RAINBOWS DANCE

My life was so dull, plain and serene
Till you came along, changing the scene
Filling me up with vibrant colours
I've never known with any other

Dancing to music of a new tune
Falling in love with the stars, the moon
Painting on a blank canvas new dreams
Wearing love poems upon my sleeve

Notes of joy filled up my dark skies
My love song reflected in your eyes
Verses flowed from pen to paper
New shades and nuances to savour

Now full are my days, warm are my nights
Your love has given me back my sight
Rainbows dance where once only rain was
You light my world with a heated flame

Copyright by Lena Power

MOMENT OF GREAT BLISS

Moment of great bliss
In aura full of cool breeze
Like morning dew on Hermon

Intense glee raptured
Us. Our love in fresh avow
I pledge to love you ever

Copyright by Fagbuaro Adedayo

SEA THOUGHTS

I am seeing you
In my heart, we are standing
At the edge of a great sea.

My hands feel you close
My breath holds you closer, but
When do you return to me.

Copyright by Paul Hudson

All that we create
in frequency of our love,
has a better taste

Copyright by Margaret Kowalewska

Two cooks one love pot
Blending love ingredients
Menu of love champions

Copyright by Marion Parish

Our hypocrisy
becomes the signs of the times
Dead men breathing ghosts

Copyright by David Wells

If you read my sign
and then read between the lines
you find my smokescreen

Copyright by Martin Gedge

Rest in bliss my dame
Let nothing fret your green dreams
Here peace do abound
Nothing unnatural frays
your course of silent repose

Copyright by Kamarudeen Mustapha

A fairy queen lies
on a green velvet carpet
Awake or asleep?
Or tranquilized by Cupid?
Her condition melts my heart

Copyright by Mafizuddin Chowdhury

Alone not lonely
My reflection surrounds me
as divinity

Copyright by Shilpa Kulkarni

We fell in the dark
Now we have become your light
just to stop your fall

Copyright by Ojotogba Ugeh

Untitled

I wish wishes
Didn't exist
I wish the world
Was woven with bliss
I wish that life
Never took nasty twists
And that prayers
We're not needed
And pain
Was a myth

I have a dream
Where dreams
Are set free
Not just for the sleeping
Or pure fantasy
But lived out
Awoken
Conscious they'd be
And nightmares just tales
That charms us in sleep...

Copyright by Patrick Reazn Dolan

THE LOVE REALM

Come inside my dear
But enter in your own risk
There's danger to get inside

Enter the love realm
Be happy or to suffer
You're safe to my heart, she said

Copyright by Ency Bearis

KISS ME

Kiss me again love.
Your kisses keep me going
until you return to me.

I wish week-ends were
longer. Then you would not be
saying goodbye to me yet.

Copyright by Ann Perry

WILD CHILD

By the guess of your dress
And the kiss of a rose
To the red of your lips
From your head to your toes
The stems of your beauty
All branches and bows
Will petal the lights of your eyes
And the garden of rain
On the flush of your face
Will grow in the soils
With the riches of grace
When you spring like a season
In this bountiful place
And forever a flower you rise.

Copyright by Martin Gedge

what can I get you?
she asked him smiling shyly
he said, can I have a date?

Copyright by Nalini Starr

Tea on the table
Kiss me if you're able to
Break that conservative air.

Copyright by Bill Noble

BREAKFAST

your smiles are tinder
a strike, my heart catches fire
hot tea for breakfast

Copyright by Ngam Emmanuel

SKIN COLORS

In the pores that rain your sadness
in the tears that drown your eyes
Like the night that falls your heavens
Like the star that falls your skies
Hold to hope that burns your sorrow
Hold to things that fill your soul
Wait for love when your tomorrow
Wait for chance when you're a go
Feel the life of your emotion
Feel the rage of your despair
Keep in mind of your devotion
Keep in sync of your repair
Let a smile to share your sun light
Let a laugh enjoy your ride
Spend the time to clear your insight
Spend to find your place outside
Wake to see your brazen glory
Wake to see your outside in
Open arms to share your beauty
Open arms to show your skin....

Copyright by Martin Gedge

Knowledgeable brain
empty mind filled with money
the best and the beast!

Copyright by Padmaja Narasimha

FOOL SPEAK

So what have you gained?
From your time of reading books?
See my coins, show yours!

Copyright by Caroline Adwar

Untitled

Autumn gems falling
To my hands... Smiling at me,
dying leaves... Soon, will
Cover earth with carpet, lush...
Embrace every change with love

Copyright by Margaret Kowalewska

BRIGHT SUN

Shall we walk the path
In the beauty of the sun?
Sister, let us laugh
While it yet lasts in the fall.
Breathing in the wild freshness.

Copyright by Caroline Adwar

SWEET NECTAR POLLINATE

Butterfly kisses
with sugar lips and honey
pretty flower girl...

Copyright by Martin Gedge

His face in her scent
Her sweet bud trembling aroused
Taste of paradise

Copyright by Margaret Kowalewska

A breath of fresh air
There, your essence lingering
Mockingly unfair this love

Keep me close for now
Breathe me in if you so dare
When winds blow my love is near.

Copyright by Jessica Perchiano

Blades of shoulders mine
Let me breathe a little life
Ebb of beginning to end

Lean there divine soul
For I waited all my life
to live and die in your arms

Copyright by Farhana Sait

Life is like a dream
With closed eyes I see our world
flow with the breeze of sunshine

As our heartbeats race
I feel like a bird in flight
drifting towards our love nest

Copyright by Omar Nassar

Brew me a nectar
from your romantic tea cup
Is life not better when shared?

Copyright by Shedrach Nwankwo

Love is like coffee
Full bodied, hot and steamy
savouring our passion drink!

Copyright by Rose Huy Woolket

Education dies
technology gains power
my knowledge declines.

Copyright by Nath Villacorte

One day you will too
dig your own grave as I do!
world always loves new!!

Copyright by Snehlata Singh

Let me dig my grave
accept the change with a smile
die in dignity

Copyright by Princess Lubna

UNTIL MY LAST BREATH

Within my notion
Upon my vision
To explore my life
I open the curtain of the future
What to see and beyond

How many years God will give me?
To wander within this wondrous world
To go along the path of life's odds
Be to unknown reckless bound
How long do I still to breathe?

My inquiry of judgement
Upon the life I'd gone through
Upon to my hobby in writing
As I offered sound of advice
Did I give enough virtues?

Within my family virtue
I did my part of fatherhood
I gave love and affection
My simple given legacy the education
And guidance to my children

Did I give enough wisdom?
Upon my presentation of poems
Within the epitome of logic
For the readers be inspired
For generation to see

Did I give a source of hope?
For the enlightenment I'd wrote
The example of legacy
What more shall I leave
Until to my last breath

Copyright by Ency Bearis

A BOYS ADVENTURE TALE

To wondering eyes
This wild boy's adventure tale
For what makes dreamers
Live and breathe in fantasy
To ignite their wilderness...

Copyright by Martin Gedge

THE PATH OF LIFE

Rejoice in your youth
We rush down the path of life
To our setting sun
When darkness covers the path
That's when we notice the stars

Copyright by Rusty Brooks

TOUCH

Could this be our final day?
When your feelings for me has swept away
Down the alley with forgotten dreams
I'll take no chances; I just want you to stay

I'll love you today like there is no tomorrow
And if someday tomorrow comes
I'll know that we gave ourselves everything
And we did all that could be done

Hold me like our hands can never touch
Wrap your arms around me as we'll never part
I know that love sometimes disappears
But I know the truth that's in my heart

I cannot imagine a love better than ours
Cannot see how I could ever replace you
So I'll love you completely every single hour
Each and every second my love I'll prove

One day I may wake up alone
But until that day you are truly my home

Copyright by Jodi Matenga

OIL FIELD

A flower shower
flaxen waxen in the sun
smile bright buttercup

Copyright by Martin Gedge

SUNSHINE

Golden bloom gleams in
Summer. Showing her beauty.
Our Earthbound sunshine.

Copyright by Ann Perry

CONFIRMING ATTRACTION

Atop the green lawn
we are lying with our books
I read, you follow along.

My mind's on your looks.
My love, is yours too, on mine?
For, if so, that would be fine.

Copyright by Fred Randall

WHENCE SILENCE SPEAKS...

Love is more a book
You read, imbibe and enjoy,
I but listen the silence.

For we, the love birds
Silence is vociferous
And a touch speaks thousand words.

Copyright by Achyut Kumar Rath

When two eyes collide
silence seems vociferous
nothing remains unspoken

Copyright Achyut Kumar Rath

Sweet lover of mine
when we kiss does your heart sing?
Mine sings so your heart hears me

Copyright Jodi Matenga

Feel your hurt my friend
I will kill you with my love
hug me while you bleed

Copyright by Poppy Nikitta Crerar

Follow the arrows
and they lead me straight to you
now I'll take a bow

Copyright by Bill Noble

The pair lost in love
She rests her head on his arm
And digests the past
Like nebulous horizon
They remain behind the shroud

Copyright by Mafizuddin Chowdhury

A beautiful day
Watching the tide rolling in
Sharing the moment
Made memories to treasure
On our favorite old bench

Copyright by James F. Cunningham

Besotted in love
Sacred souls coming closer
In the nature's lap
In tranquillity they sing
The song of eternal love

Copyright by Tulsidas Satpathy

Untitled

It was love that burned
From the earth to the heavens
As they soared the sky
Literally swept away
She received his proposal.

Copyright by Priscilla Light

A LOVE NOT LIKE SUNSET

I ask for a love
A love that's not like sunset
It fades over time
What a beauty one can watch
Yet painful and heartbreaking

Copyright by JB Ignalangin

On pale branches, death
Hangs fragile limbs like sick leaves
Praying for the sun

Copyright by Nnane Ntube

AUTUMN NIGHT

moonbeams spatter shine
as autumn leaves gently fall
trees in delight bask

Copyright by Ngam Emmanuel

GROUND CONTROL

Drifting through this atmosphere
a first for all mankind
Checked our path the coast is clear
Is Houston on the line?
We traveled far this distant star
To bold where seldom go
A capsule round this space age town
As we go to rockets slow
We're a million miles from the sun
And 4 weeks from my home
We reach the base to start the phase
To breach the outer zone
Upon decent this message sent
I hope you can relate
A failure is not an option here
We must communicate
We're on a trek as we expect
Our destination close
From outer space to ground control
Let's raise a glass and toast
It's history for all to see
And we welcome to the room
A camera shot of an astronaut
As we step on to the moon...

Copyright by Martin Gedge

THE SPIRIT OF FLYING EAGLE

Close your eyes to feel your heart
And let the soul release
Raise your arms to spread your wings
And find that inner peace
Deep inside the wind to glide
Just let the breezes blow
Then to the air where angels dare
You're there before you know
Across the sky as eagles fly
Beneath the golden suite
The crystal blue and ocean view
Beneath your starry feet
And over trees like flower bees
You groom the mountains high
Through valleys low where rivers flow
You watch the world go by
And from above your inner love
Will paint a perfect scene
And open eyes will realize
Your spirit is your dream

Copyright by Martin Gedge

Damn my ugly fate
my progress in life is slow
when I want to grow

Copyright by Omar Nassar

TIME TO TIME

To time we rise up
We're grains of sand in hourglass
We fall with the time

Copyright by Ency Bearis

Untitled

I remember when
we kissed under the full moon
before you passed from this earth

my lips still taste yours
the memory of us lives
in the romance of my heart

Copyright by Kailash Magar

FOCUS

It was the focus
The blossoming light of one
The origins of true love

In a field of blur
Witnesses spill undefined
Linger long after the bud

Copyright by David Wells

TRUTH NEVER TOLD

She dreams eyes open
Visions of an earthly kind
The cub dreams eyes closed
Both see beauty in the mind
Truth revealed but never told

Copyright John Herlihy

MOTHER SON

Visions of grandeur
Vast worlds of hope you shall seek
Run wild mother son
Be at well of life from cub
To king and to crown a throne

Copyright Martin Gedge

Standing at portal
to reach out to you my love
my password is obsession

Copyright Sudha Dixit

Our balmy embrace
like an aperitif leads
us to the sumptuous banquet

Copyright Ngam Emmanuel

ANGEL TEARS

Angel tears fall down
To shine as rain drops on leaves
Sprinkles down with breeze
Creates stream to succour life
Nature's pleasant lullaby

Copyright Purbasha Roy

UNTITLED

Glistening dewdrops
Shimmers in the rising dawn
Slowly burn away
Natures amazing beauty
Tantalizing your senses

Copyright James F. Cunningham

If time is treasure
we rob the one we love
with total strangers

Copyright by Rusty Brooks

Do not twitter me!
it drives me completely mad
online madness rules

Copyright by Ann Perry

In this freezing breeze
I can't just watch my kids freeze
I must get some food
No matter what it will take
To fly from my vantage stake

Copyright by Omar Nassar

Sweet red-breasted bird
Your gentle singing is heard
In the Winter Chill
Perching on wooden fencing
Awaiting the warmth of Spring

Copyright by Ann Perry

My sun was waning
until the Phoenix arose
to alight the dusk.

Copyright by Barney Cissell

Art thou not twilight?
day time not thou night time too
footstep in between.

Copyright by Hamzu Hamza

RED ROSE

Nature's sweetest kiss
With red luscious perfumed lips
Hallmark of true love

Copyright by Namita Rani Panda

Wrinkles smooth as dust
Fragile folds of crimson blush
Dipped in bloom of lust

Copyright by David Wells

RED ROSE

PEACEKEEPER

My days as a peacekeeper are over.
Duties for King and Country are done.
I'm coming home to you my love.
There's peace now. It's time for fun.

I don't want to dwell on the things that I saw.
The bloodshed, the misery, the death.
I don't want to ask, 'what was it all for?'
The given answers will never impress.

Too many are not coming back with me.
We are leaving them far from home.
Most will have names and a family.
But some will remain unknown.

Will there ever really be 'Peace in Our Time?'
Isn't that what they said?
It's what we strive for again and again.
But soldiers are still ending up dead.

Copyright by Ann Perry

Angel of the sky
Spreads peaceful wings so high
His heart is a temple
A dwelling place of innocence
Into heaven's calmness he flies

Copyright by Nnane Ntube

SOAR HIGH

Like an eagle spread your wings, soar
Let the wind take you gliding high
There, where the wuthering winds blow
Where crimson clouds rage thru the sky
Let your heart sing, your passions fly

Copyright by Renette Dsouza

IGNITE

Stay away, don't get too close,
Steer clear; we'd communicate through a hose.

Once you're near, I'm finished.
You create in me strongholds that to my willpower diminish.
Whether I become senseless or breathless, I barely can distinguish,
But it leaves me satisfied as when treated to a savoury dish.
Yet I want you away,
As yonder as me in the ocean, and you at bay,
For with just a tad approach, we'd bond like clay.
So near me not, though my heart is in utter dismay.
My mind tells me I'm being too hard,
My body confirms the remark.
Oh, I'm lost...in quagmire island.

I yearn for you, but I fear for me.
You ignite in my feelings so wild,
A blazing inferno, I fear I'd get scald.
But amidst the fears that shroud my heart,
The compulsion is raging, to play my part...
My part of facing my fears by taking a step closer...
If I die, I die....the phobia is over.
I hasten my pace, as I see you do the same towards me.
Seems you knew I'd make this decision.
So I race to you with all fractions of might,
And we lock in an embrace so tight.
I realize in amazement, that I didn't get burnt,
I instead, experienced a rebirth,
Just like a Phoenix...
For I'm fazed no more by fearful hoaxes.

Copyright by Ruth Anya Kālu

COSMIC EMBRACE

Your arms are my world, my cosmos.
Your heartbeat is source of my conscious.

I'm getting lost in your universe.
When you hold me this very close.
Millions of stars I see through your eyes.
Enlightened I'm entering outer space.

You are my billions of light years.
I have to research all your galaxies.
Somewhere inside the secret exists.
Your embrace life's meaning reveals.

Copyright by Alla Arthur .

FORTUNE

A twist of fate plunging to serendipity,

Mode of nature complimenting sincerity,

Triumph with dedication touch successfully,

Fortunate is one who lived with honesty.

Born once with life of challenges,

Perseverance rewarded the better changes,

Destiny too changed with prayers,

Fortune is made with your own hands!

Copyrights reserved Farhana Sait

Pillars of Creation

Far beyond our thoughts could think
Give birth to stars that shine with bliss
It was called pillars of creation
Where galaxies born and all constellations...

Stars may live a trillion years
But they too will die in due season
In total darkness they will be thrown
To sink in an unending black hole...

Stars may rise and soar today
But tomorrow they'll fade away
Out comes a new born celebrity
To replace glittering gem of yesterday.

Give new stars chance to fly
If you've reached your ultimate shine
At least you have memories to cherish
That once, you soared above the rest...

Copyright by Lovely Garcia
Publisher/ Admin/Founder

The Unknown, Everyday Heroes

Another day at the station,
Just doing routine daily chores.
Checking the gear and washing the trucks,
Cleaning counters, toilets, and floors.

Talks, jokes, and teamwork all around,
A brotherhood that's tried and true,
A true family though not kin by blood,
Friendships that is hard to outdo.

The tones are alerted, alarms are sounded.
They jump into action, ready to go
No matter what the call is
Or the weather - sun, rain or snow.

It may be a car accident
With people hurt and trapped inside
Or maybe a medical call -
Unfortunately, they died.

It may be trees that have fallen,
Or maybe power lines down,
Or a house that is on fire -
They tried but it burned to the ground.

Firefighters are priceless.
For without them, we would fall apart.
They do their jobs with humbleness,
Putting in every bit of their hearts.

They take each back with them,
Asking if they could have made a change.
And if a change was made,
Would it have mattered long range.

They carry happiness
For the calls that went well;
So, hopefully they will not
In the bad and traumatic calls dwell.

Citizens will never know
What it costs a firefighter

To do the job they love to do.
So, try to make their world brighter.

Stop complaining about petty things.
Appreciation goes a long way.
Speak to them in the community.
Do things that will brighten their day.

The unknown, everyday heroes,
Doing their jobs with unsung praise.
I hope you do not need to call for
Them one of these days.

© Christy Hall-Hollowell
Moderator/Game Conductor

SURRENDER

I hid beneath
Love to shelter
Myself from
Turbulent tides

It's easy
To fall when
Struggle shuns
My attempt to rise

No denying
Life is beautiful
But nobody teaches
Living isn't a joy ride

So I surrender
To the universe
Swaying along its tunes
In God's grace, my being smiles.

Copyright by Tanushi Singh
Moderator/Game Conductor

IF

If my heart stops
I'll see you
Beyond the realm
Of understanding
Our Now

If we part ways
I'll meet you
Beyond the realm
Of questioning
Our why or how

If we don't remain we
Then I'll rest in peace
Knowing I was loved
My heart might stop
But the soul will carry on

Copyright by Tanushi Singh

WORDSMITH

A dizzy dawn
A fiddly question
Burst in my brain
What is a poet
A while I was quiet
Then I started
Poet is a builder
He is an engineer
Using piles of words
And bricks of phrases
Using emotions
He joins the pieces
And builds dreams
Goldsmith certifies
Gold as he identifies
Emotions and words
His nib as people says
Is mightier than swords
He is a Smith of words
Call him a wordsmith
A chore he was born with.

Copyright by Saswat Kumar Mishra
Official Graphic Artist

A Beautiful Soul

B ehind my story and different journey
E ach has its unique reason and wonderful lesson
A tale to remember and to keep forever
U ntold story to hear and to share
T o touch one's heart and one's soul
I t is a hundred poems about life, hope and love
F or you to believe and not to give up
U nveil the fears and cast away the doubts
L ive life, live moments and be happy

S omehow, there is one man who inspired me
O ne man that taught me to love unconditionally
U nknowing the answer but be just
L eaving to time and fate as long as my beautiful soul lives

Copyright by Marites Tordecilla
Moderator/Game Conductor

Published by Marites Ritumalta / Lovely Garcia
Designed and compiled by Lovely Garcia
Edited by Lovely Garcia
Cover Artist: dagat Payapa
Back Cover Photo: Pinterest

www.ingramcontent.com/pod-product-compliance
Lightning Source LLC
LaVergne TN
LVHW062355180726
843498LV00008B/1317